SHE LET HERSELF GO

SHE LET HERSELF GO

poems

George Ella Lyon

LOUISIANA STATE UNIVERSITY PRESS
BATON ROUGE

Published by Louisiana State University Press
Copyright © 2012 by George Ella Lyon
All rights reserved
Manufactured in the United States of America
LSU Press Paperback Original
First printing

DESIGNER: Michelle A. Neustrom
TYPEFACE: MrsEaves
PRINTER AND BINDER: IBT Global

LIBRARY OF CONGRESS CATALOGING-IN-PUBLICATION DATA

Lyon, George Ella, 1949–
   She let herself go : poems / George Ella Lyon.
     p. cm.
   ISBN 978-0-8071-4276-9 (pbk. : alk. paper) — ISBN 978-0-8071-4278-3 (epub)
— ISBN 978-0-8071-4277-6 (pdf) — ISBN 978-0-8071-4279-0 (mobi)
   I. Title.
   PS3562.Y4454S47 2012
   811'.54—dc23

                                                          2011033091

The author offers grateful acknowledgment to the editors of the following publications
where these poems originally appeared:

The American Voice: "Strung"; *Appalachian Heritage:* "Receiving," "My Dearest Darling," "If I
could find," and "In the Balance"; *Appalachian Journal:* "All"; *Back: Poems:* "The Baby Bed";
Catapla: "To the Lighthouse"; *Cries of the Spirit:* "Inventing Sin"; *Discover Art in Kentucky:* "With
a Song in His Heart"; *Earth Poems:* "Oak"; *Hiram Poetry Review:* "The Edge of Night"; *Iron
Mountain Review:* "Four Stone Steps"; *Journal of Kentucky Studies:* "Meeting the Notebook";
Larkspur Press and *Appalachian Journal:* "Prayer"; *Limestone:* "Just Might" and "Yes!"; *Motif 1:
Writing by Ear:* "Mary"; *New Works Review, Online Edition:* "No Blanket but Stars"; *Pine Mountain
Sand & Gravel:* "Love over Physics"; *Seminary Ridge Review:* "Eve of Winter"; *Where I'm From,
Where Poems Come From:* "This Kitchen Floor"; *Wind:* "Morning" and "Temple Bells";
Woolfwork: "At Talland House," "To Say Nothing of Your Face," and "To Virginia."

For all the writing communities who have sustained and shaped my work,

> *from Roberta White's poetry group at Centre College*
> *to Ruth Stone's at Indiana University*
> *to Gurney Norman's through the Appalachian Poetry Project*
> *to the ever-expanding one created by the Kentucky Women Writers Conference*
> *and the far-flung literary circle centered in the Appalachian Writers Workshop*
> > *at Hindman Settlement School.*

My love and thanks to you all.

It takes villages!

CONTENTS

SHE LET HERSELF GO

STRUNG

on muscle
of myth and miracle
a uterine knot
of work and words
I put down the pen
its uncapped nib
staining the blotter.

Colossus of rose
I step across
the African violet
blooming in my study
to open the window
and let in April's
feast of emergence.

Below, the clothesline
high-strung, empty
waits for the nightgown
soaking in the basement
waits while blood words
rise from the cloth
through the great white-out
of bleach.

Revise me, April.
I am forty-five
blue lines like veins
on the page of my skin
and this red thread
for all its strength
fades to an end.

Give me word-root
umbilical of ink
to bear me up

when the tying-off comes
of the line that is
my mother's

mother's

mother's

to all the crowning heads
of woman's estate.

YES!

She had the nerve, the gall,
the eggs, the guts, the chutzpa
to say it. She said it. She will say it
in front of God and furniture, neighbors
and senior wardens. Her hair
is bright, her eyes wide, and the purple
sparkle of her toenails dazzles.
She stands up short, tall, full-bodied,
willowy, her rugged hands graceful
as lilies, spotted as trout, and she
says, in a voice that still will sing
the birth of the world, she says NO.

IN MY DREAM

In my dream I reach for your hand.
You reach too, grasping mine with an intake of breath.
I want to fold you in my arms and let blackness blanket us.

In my dream you walk up and kiss me
as though I were a statue you were bringing to life.
Lightly you say, "Let's not look back."

In my dream
In my dream

In my dream I kiss the palm of your hand
and petals fly from your fingertips.
Stones roll from the road. The way is clear.

Birds chirp between my legs and I am a tree,
a crotch of promise. A tough membrane
and a thin shell between tomorrow and song.

Let jubilation take us.

MIRROR, MIRROR

She is jealous, this crone,
of the maiden, Snow White.
She means to kill her.
Skull-tight hood
ice-white face
black cape alive
with daggers.
She will try a poison apple—
beauty for beauty.
It won't work.

Life is on the girl's side:
the well
the apple tree
the dwarfs—
all want Snow White
to live and flourish.
But first she has to walk
the dark forest
eat the fruit, fall
under the spell.
That's just how it goes.
Heigh-Ho, Heigh-Ho.

LOVE OVER PHYSICS

—With thanks to Barry Parker's
Cosmic Time Travel

O, for a balm
to coat the wormhole in time,
some exotic matter
to lather against the twist
of that hourless glass

that I might navigate
the outer event horizon
the inner event horizon
and even the singularity

without being strung out
without being pinched off

but, clutching whatever gifts
I might glean from this present,
careen through another universe
straight to you.

HONESTLY

Zeus, that big flirt,
went after a mortal today.
As a swan, if you can believe
it. Leda somebody. Mortals
for my money are more trouble
than they're worth. Zeus too.
But I've served up a lot of ambrosia
since I tied the knot with Old Thunderbolt.
Till death do us part, you know, which it won't.

OH WELL

They didn't live happily
but then they didn't live ever after either.

SOME BIG LOUD WOMAN

I need some big loud woman to listen to
        Orangey red
   Wild-haired
Her voice like
        A waterfall of kettles
Her head back   eyes shut
    Back arched
To roar that music out

I need the brass and bramble
    Of her low notes
The trembling windows
    Of her high

Bare feet planted on the floorboards
Green dress a summer canopy

The wail in one line
A scar on the air

I need to listen to a big loud woman
Heavy fists
     Pounding on my table
Her anger
     Fire in the hearth

I need the avalanche
        of her laughter
the flood
        of her truth

I need to listen
    To some big loud woman

I need some big loud woman to listen to

NO BLANKET BUT STARS

He was born
where things meet
at the red rock
the right place
in swift pain
my sister with me
and a mother
of our mother's line
to cut the cord

He is welcome
who walked
with the Spirit
and grew
in darkness
and danced
to my heart's drum

He is cradled
in a basket
and no wish
no hope   no fear
widens our eyes
All is complete

I know the wheel
turns   Tomorrow
we must leave
the red rock
return to our people
This first one
will outgrow
the basket   my milk
He will walk away
to meet blood-words

But for now
I almost see
the hoop
that holds us
like the basket
It shines
at all the edges
of the world

ALL THAT LIGHT

You were a month late, we say,
as if you'd been goofing off
in the womb while your father

and I were all dressed and ready.
We did have the handmade
cradle set at the foot of the bed

and a little chest of gowns, bibs,
and blankets. We did have
my grandmother's rocker

and a battery-powered lamp
and a plastic tub like a boat.
But we didn't have a clue

about you—fierce spirit
waiting to wake us up to what
we'd rather sleep through,

to open with new hands
all those selves we'd put a lid on.
O Hermes, held back so long

you had to wear corrective
shoes: you were late, we say
swaddling in our Shadows

all that light.

RECEIVING

I had no idea how to hold a baby.
Forget instinct. It doesn't feel like it looks.
And you were a squirmer and wouldn't
stay swaddled. "Receiving blankets"
we called those cloths you threw off,
as though we'd held them stretched
beneath stars while you fell from heaven.
In the yellow one with rabbits stamped on,
I wrapped you for our first trip out.
You wriggled and stretched and fought
with fists when I held you in the crook
of my arm. Laid on my shoulder, you bellied
around like a snake. It was September.
Hot. Hot. And you smothered
in a drawstring gown and that
blanket. I didn't have a grip.
That much was clear. And you were on
your journey, in search of something firmer
or freer. I still do not know which.

JUST MIGHT

If Persephone wants to waltz off after flowers
the very place I told her not to go
and get herself dragged by her pretty little foot
down to Hades, well, let her. I was wild for a while,
I'll admit, running all over creation
calling her name, but I'm past it. Girls
will be girls. Pluto's got her? Um-hmm.
Then he's got his shady hands full. And anyway,
two can play that game.

My move is to quit. As of this bean. No more seed
and sprout and harvest. No more golden ears
plumping green shocks. What a relief!
All that blooming! The constant shitwork.
Pushing asparagus out of the ground
a foot a day—my god, I can't believe I did it.

But for your kids, you'll do anything, right? And it
used to work. It balanced out. Then Hermes stole
those cows, and every kid since has thought she had
to trespass big time to get her version of sandals
and a winged hat. Never mind the cost. So my girl's
gone to Hell like the rest of them. Well, well. The world
can dry up and blow away as long as Persephone gets
her flowers, her pomegranate seeds. As her mother,
I can tell you: it just might.

ADORATION

I scrub the tub, all the time thinking
it is an oval of heaven. Here I bathed
my baby lord's feet, here I washed
his milkweed hair and with a soapy
rag traveled the round mound of him.
As promised. As pledged in the dark
one February night, cooking up
lovers' delight, stirring
in my soft vessel someone new.
Someone grown now, the sky riding
his shoulders, the vault of heaven
above him, which only the wind scrubs.

THE BABY BED

In my parents' bedroom my baby bed
has reappeared and a radiant figure stands
in the door. Something is urging me
to look under their bed. A clear voice
says I shouldn't do this, but it is weaker
than the force like a hand on the back
of my neck. In a second, I am belly-down
on the blue carpet, slithering under the rail.

What should I see but a rose-rock canyon
and me, a small naked boy, on a ledge
halfway down? I *see* him, then I am
swallowed into him. My skin is the same hue
as the stone, my hair crow-black. I am
not yet three and my heart is stricken.
How could they leave me? Where did they all go?
There's a ladder but I'm too small to climb.
I crouch down beside a huge pot to have something
to be next to. I see red ochre drawings on the wall.
Then I close my eyes
                        and the canyon changes.
Lush green, the rock now gray-silver-black. Again
I'm a naked child, this time a girl and older, maybe five.
Again I'm on a ledge halfway down. Everything is wet,
breathing steam. Below me, canopies of trees. I know
I know I know all my people have been killed.
There is no one to care for me. What food we had is gone
and I can't escape this ledge to find more. I look up
and see, on the green-fringed top of the cliff, soldiers.
They don't look like me. They have lowered a net over
the cliff and want me to climb. I ask my bones if this is a trap.
They do not know. I ask my belly if I will be their food.
Only hunger answers. It's clear that here I will die,
up there I might not. So I climb, watching their spotty
clothes, streaked faces, helmets and guns get closer.
Then hands grab my arms, haul me up, and on a rise

behind them, I see my yellow-white crib. They set me
in it, hoist it to their shoulders and carry me
through the jungle. Safe.

And I am once again my grown self
in my parents' bedroom. Another force
draws me downstairs, past the turn and the library,
down another flight through the hall toward
the basement stairs. *No No No,* something says,
but I keep going, a grappling hook in my belly,
its line reeling me in.
                        Beyond the basement door,
at a desk where the stoker used to be, sits my father
twenty years dead, hard at work. I want to talk, but he
is too busy. My heart hurts. "Tell your mother I'll
be there soon," he says, dismissive. I shift my weight
to my heel to leave but then step forward. "I wish
you had been here more," I tell my smoke-wreathed
daddy. "I wish you weren't always at work."
He looks up at me, his eyes bright blue. I feel him
start to speak anger, then change course. He puts
his head on his arms on the desk. "I do, too," he says.
I lean forward, reaching to touch him, but the desk
and Daddy become a tapestry of leaves. When I pull
my hand back, they reappear. This time I walk
to the side of the desk, lean down and hug him.
"I love you," I say. He returns the words.
                              And I am
a young man climbing a steep forest path. My neck
aches from a pole laid across it. I am carrying
something hung from each end of the pole, heavy
as water. Above and to the left I see a temple—
an open-air pagoda, with red-lacquered poles raising
a red gold-kissed roof. When I reach the entrance, I set
my burden down. But just before I step into incense
and chanting I look over my right shoulder where the path
continues its ascent. There at the top is my baby bed
glowing. More. There is more to be born.

ALL HALLOW'S EVE

—For my father

I got your mouth. Each day I line those full lips, color in
your smile. I'd hoped for your sweetness, too, but my son got that.
Once when I was little, sitting on your Nu-Way Cleaners counter,
Col. Perkins came in, saw us together and said, "Bob, while she lives,
you'll never die." Since then fifty years have vanished
like spots you lifted from the garments of our small town,
standing on concrete at your stainless steel board, mesh-topped
to let caustic juices through. Except what caught beneath your ring,
ethered into your cells. Col. Perkins is long gone, the cleaners too,
and you laid to rest for nineteen years. You'd been to medical school.
You knew about death's grim solvent. It's Halloween. Give us
a smile, Daddy. You loved handing candy to a flock of ghosts.

SHAKE

I don't know, I don't know what makes me shake like this. It's made me so thin, too. That dress you always loved—blue and green with the scooped neckline—it hangs on me now. In fact, I'm shaking so I can barely see it. Maybe the blue is really sky, the green what I remember of leaves. But if so, how did the tree branches turn white, like my arms?

Telllllll mmmmeeeee. Am I cold, shaking cold? Am I effervescent? Where is the slow garment that was my days? I seem to just be here. Hhhhheeeeerrrrre. And tethered. Is there a joke forever funny and I'm laughing myself to death? Is this fear—night sky jerking, stars rattling, constellations tumbling like white-in-black dice?

Ohohoh and my numb numb numbers are uhuhppp. So so so lllet mme go. These toes, elbows, shoulders, these knees, these me's. I am not happy. Listen. I am all motion, no joy. A leaf blazes, thins out and dies, rattles and then rides the air. Rests elsewhere. Unhitch me from the surge of your need and let me fly apart, lie in particles. I can get along without me. You can too.

MORNING

I am
remembered
by something
from before
I took
this form

as if in sleep
I crossed
to where
the soul
knows all
its stories

and now
though time's
light beckons
I cannot
quite
cross back.

HALF A CHANCE

The dream self knows
and tries to tell
Every night
she takes me to the movies
See? See? she says
That's us
the ballerina with the tattoo
the boy eating feathers
the liar
the murderer
the old lady with beans in her ears
Don't you get it
Would you put down that popcorn
And I say
I need my sleep

What you mean, she says
is you'd like to be
even less conscious in the dark
than in the light
Well, forget it
You only give me
six hours a night
and I'm not about to let you stay
as numb and dumb as you are
in the day
Don't you understand
We've got work to do

There's those dead people in the basement
you need to look at
Are you ever going to go down there
in the middle of a Wednesday afternoon
I don't think so

There's the angel you need to kiss
the devil to dandle on your knee
And what about the little bones
snapped into cassette boxes
and kept in the library
on the lowest self—
who will get you to look at them
Not the kid at the drivethru
with the french fries
Not the Orkin man

Now remember when I took you
to the barren field
that was also your old neighborhood
and gave you a bomb
like the Orkin man's poison can
Remember how heavy it was
smooth and silver
like a hard bright baby dirigible
in your arms
and you couldn't put it down
and you wandered the streets
the waste places
frantic with fear
who could you give it to
when would the holocaust come

But the daybell rang
and you slammed the dream door
and zipped your prodigious anger
into another pair of bargain pants
put on your favorite earrings
and went about your day
which wasn't about your life at all
and left me dumbfounded
and asking myself

what the hell
what the heaven
what the upper world
    lower world
        Hades and bardo

could I show you
that might get through
next time you lie down
close those blind eyes
and give me
half a chance

TALKING IN THE BASEMENT

I want to know what
you're doing down here,
Daddy. You're supposed
to be at Resthaven, where
we buried you in '86
but I come down to the
basement, after sorting
electrical wires with
Mother, after listening
to her quarrel with Black
Holes, and find you, no
shirt, sweaty and dirty
as a dockhand, sitting
in a golden oak desk chair,
probably from your office
at the drycleaner's, looking
overworked but in your
prime. I am stunned.
You're in the room that
used to be the coal bin: all
dirt since you converted
to oil. The chute's boarded
over, the shelf of earth where
a litany of cats had their
kittens is strewn with
rusty tools. I stare at you.
You're glistening—so physical.
"Of course I've been here," you
say. "Where else could I go?"
"Heaven?" I offer. You laugh.
The chair creaks. "I've been
meaning to write you a letter,"
you tell me. "There's
something I need to say."
Me, too, but it lies on my
tongue like ash left so long

in the furnace it overwhelms
the fire. I don't say
anything. I don't see the bed-
side commode someone tossed
in the dark corner. Only you,
radiant and impatient, who
have work to do

LIFE SENTENCE

—For Christine Banks Lyon

Shuffling, no longer able
to lift your feet
holding my hand like
a lover or a child
you walked with me
around the fenced-in grounds
of the Glasgow State Nursing Facility.

Brain tangles had webbed away
light from your eyes
order from your thoughts
the name of my husband,
your only child, from your tongue.
You no longer greeted him with
"Oh, there you are!" No longer
pretended to cook his supper
at the nurse's station. The only
sign of the life-fire that had once
danced between you was a slight
softening of the Alzheimer's mask
when he came into view.

Images swirled in my mind
as we stepped our slow way—

the Christmas you gave me
that rose and gray kimono

your long alcoholic evenings
in the townhouse in Miami

your high school football-star
fiancé who died in the victory bonfire

the heather-blue dress you knitted
before we met and wore
in a glamour shot with Bud
dearest husband enemy
at some racetrack

                        the pink
and purple that orchids spoke
from fence and trees and pots
in your tiny backyard garden.

I was parsing what I knew
of the life sentence
of one who would never speak
a coherent thought again
when you halted our snail's
round, turned your stiff sturdy
body to mine and asked,
"Where did I put them,
all my magnificent tomorrows?"

TEMPLE BELLS

It was my father, setting
me on the stone wall,
giving me a drink with petals
floating in it.
It was him bowing,
then turning to walk the path
and disappear. It was
my mother, raking the sand
of the yard, sweeping the terrace,
keeping her face stone.
It was putting my tongue
to the cool belly of the copper
bowl, its taste like
blood-water. It
was crying. It was
Mother breaking bamboo
before my eyes, saying
You will eat.
You will not
cry. It was fish
paste, salty, viscous.
It was napping in the hot
afternoon and dreaming
of rolling down a hill, a purple
shawl of mist billowing
around me. It was
the sun at the bottom of the hill
in a tent. It was waking
and drawing my dream in the sand,
then showing Mother, whose
face softened as she said
the word *Pavillion*.
It was my father turning
to disappear. It was
temple bells calling.

AT THE WELSH
FOLKLIFE MUSEUM

I was alone
when I saw it:
the deep red
stucco house
with a rowan
tree, Our Lady
of the Mountain,
keeping evil
from the yard.

Among tourists
was there another
whose heart leapt
when they lifted
the latch, who
knew the thick
white-washed walls
the door would
open into?

Climbing steep
boxed-in stairs
I could barely
breathe for what
I knew I'd find:
the narrow room
where once stars
drew close as I
gave birth.

TREE VALENTINE

To be with trees
on the path
to lay your hand
on the smooth bark of a beech
and feel its lifework
sap and water flowing
through the cambium
just beneath your palm
a continuous relay
up through drinking roots
down through breathing leaves
to thicken the trunk
add to the bark
rework, reweave, grow

Such deep peace
as you find
among oak and birch
hickory and fir
is not resting
but the steady pulse
of running a channel of life
between dirt and stars
praying through
bud bloom fruit seed
for the ongoing of forest
for flicker honeybee
weasel trout lily
all day all night
lifting open branches
heat sleet hail howling wind
Soul bridges stand
all around you
Leave a gift in the roots
Touch wood

If I could find my

edges, I might be able

to work my puzzle.

ALL

—For my grandmother
Ruby May Lane Fowler
1898–1969

She bore her life.
She took it all—
Those years she was a slip of a Memphis girl
Carrying her sheet music in a suede roll
Running off by train with a timber man
Setting up housekeeping in one scraped-out
Mountain town after another

Fifteen years pregnant or nursing
That slip grown thick
The way a tree wears its time
Her temper turned fierce
By the endlessness
Of mouths to feed
Bottoms to wipe
Clothes to wash and starch and sew
Cows to milk gardens to hoe

She bore it all
Jack, the baby fever shook the life from
Mickey, the little girl who broke
The choke-hold of diphtheria
Only to be crushed in a car at fifteen
Lane, her firstborn, "Little Son" they called him
Whose heart seized up
As he shaved for church
And felled him like a tree at forty-three

And Dave, that rail of a handsome boy
She caught the train with,
That lean man in khaki work clothes
Whose sawmills she followed

From holler to coal town to county seat
She bore him
Laid out on sawdust
At Clyde Gaines's mill
Where he'd gone on a Monday morning's business
She bore handing her house key
To strangers
Living alone above the drycleaners
Broiling her little piece of lean meat
Eating her dry potato
Because of her weight, you see,
Because of her heart
She bore it all—
The life that came to her
The man who carried her away
The children time made of them
The crush of those crazy-quilt years
The clock-tick aloneness at the end

With an iron will
A sharp wit
And a good foundation garment
She bore her life
Seventy-one years
Then laid it down
One July afternoon
In the Harlan Appalachian Regional Hospital
Leaving behind
Four children
Thirteen grandchildren
Four gleaming rooms
All these stories.

MY DEAREST DARLING

—Poem found in my grandfather's letter

Cubage, Ky
Aug. 22, 1916

Miss Josie Wilder

Oaks, Ky

My Dearest Darling.
I will now with pleasure
ans. your letter
rec= Saturday and was
so glad to get another.

Darling you are all
I have to think about
and I am so hapy it
don't Seam as I ever
will See any more trouble
Sence I have some one that
Says they will love me always.

There is no time I will ever
injoy like I did Sunday evening
with out I am with you.
And I new if I ever talk
with you I would love you to
well. . . . I can't be satisfide
any more away from you
my Darling. . . . Good lovers
together is all the
injoyment on this earth.

Dear all is gone to bed
while I am sitting here
writing my Darling girl,
injoying the time not thinking

of Sleep. For there is nothing
bothers me for all my study
is just you.

So be good Darling till
we meet again and that will
be Sunday if I am living.
Wrote with love and best wish
      forever yours
          Robert Hoskins

ans soon)

WHICH IS WHY

Married in
the mountains
in the morn-
ing they drove
bad roads to
Lexington
good roads to
Cincinnati
to get to
Crosley Field
in time to
see the Reds
in a double
header their
wedding night
which is why
there was no
reception
there are no
pictures not
even of
their supper—
red hots and
coffee—or
the dream come
true after
the game when
they stood in
line down by
the bullpen
and Mother
offered Diz-
zy Dean her
program for
the swift and

thrilling flou-
rish of his pen
the kiss of his
autograph.

AFRICAN VIOLETS

—With thanks to Charlotte Nolan

That's the bed, right there, where she all but lived those last few
years. Had her African violets—yes, honey, right on the *quilt*—her
Bible, of course, her Sunday School paper and church bulletin, throat
lozenges. Let's see, what else? Pictures of the kids and grandkids,
medicines—no, in the *bed* with her, I'm telling you. Fussed and fumed if
I tried to take them out.

Had her liniment bottle, her Hadacol, her reading glasses, two or
three library books, and a brace of old *Reader's Digests*. It's a wonder she
didn't get bedsores from not having enough room to turn over. When
one of her violets turned a really peculiar shade of purple I accused her
of pouring the Hadacol to it. I still think maybe she did.

Did I say she had her pocketbook with her coin purse and lotion,
lipstick and mirror, and earbobs in case the preacher came? Why honey,
this bed was a whole damn train compartment! And she died right here—
rode it to the end of the line.

DIVING LESSON

"I'll teach her!" my uncle said,
putting his hot hairy hands
on my shoulders and turning me
around. I faced the pool:
the wide wobble of water, all
splashing laughter, glistening limbs.
He marched me across rough
concrete to the smooth plank.

"Go on," he said. "I'm right here."
In the Big One, he'd been
on a hospital ship in the Pacific.
Water and a little girl's fear
were nothing to him.
                              I climbed
up, inched out, with my uncle
right behind me, till I reached
the edge, felt the spring, began
to shake. He put his hand
on the nape of my neck and pushed.
I resisted. "Bend over!" he barked
and I did. Then he knelt,
grasped my ankles, pinned
my feet. "Fall forward!"
he ordered, but I froze. "This
is the LOW board, damn it!
You've barely got an inch
to fall!" Still I stayed jack-
knifed. So, anchoring my ankles
with one hand, he pushed
my hips forward with the other,
then began his lecture on how
to dive.
              The trouble was, he was
right: the board was low.
My head, from crown to chin,

was submerged. Above me,
my uncle's voice bubbled on.
I couldn't scream, free my feet,
lift my spine, just tore
at the water with wild hands

until a huge plunge rocked
my prison, an arm hooked
my body and pulled me free.
Some high school boy laid
me down by the ladder
and pushed drowning out
while my uncle swore.

MOTHER OF PEARL

Your wedding gift
A real strand
Real
Despite the war
And Daddy's vision
Which meant he couldn't be
A doctor, had to be
A drycleaner

Those true-to-the-tooth-test orbs
Born of invasive irritation
That you wore to the Margie Grand
Where the two of you
Newlyweds
Held hands all through
Sergeant York
Until your free fingers
Sought the pearls and found
Nothing.

Frantic, you felt
The sticky floor
Beneath, around, in front of
Your seats
And when the show was over
Threaded the rows, needling
Every nook with the usher's
Flashlight, but found
Not one glowing ○
No string, no clasp, no
Evidence of love's extravagance
Once offered on black
Velvet, now cascaded
Into deeper dark.

FOUND

—For Roe

We
were teenagers
together, got married
had our babies alongside
one another. We lost our
fathers together, and now
we navigate our
mothers' old
age

We
sang Elvis
together, "Wise men
say . . . ," poured our hearts
out to each other, borrowed
one another's skirts and
on heavy days
bled on
them

We
were best
cousins and didn't
kill ourselves though we
tried. We must have lost
our mothers in some
war history didn't
notice, doesn't
mention

Now
we are
as old as
the speed limit on

a two-lane road. Your
heart almost threw a
rod, I'm out
of alignment,
we

travel,
our history
a guidebook we
will not give the
children, but here is our
story: when we were
most lost we
found each
other

THIS KITCHEN FLOOR

When my mother wanted us
        to go to Europe
on a special deal
        with my brother's senior class
her mother said
        how can you spend the money
with this kitchen floor
        gone crumbly and soft?

and my mother said
        when my children are grown
they'll remember Europe
        they won't remember this floor

but I do   thirty years

its deep blue border
        like the cobalt sky
        one night over Venice
its marbleized swirls
        of indigo and snow
        cerulean and pitch
rich as the rim
        of the baptismal font
in the shadows
        of Saint-Germain-des-Prés.

WITH A SONG IN HIS HEART

Daddy called the Walkman
his play-pretty and he loved it

like he loved the radio
that sang him to sleep.

(Mother listened to talk
shows. They had

pillow speakers.) He loved
the radio like he loved

the hi-fi with Mario Lanza's
heart breaking in his voice

or the Beatles looping "Let
It Be" on the eight-track

like he loved my brother
always at the spinet and later

the grand piano striking
heart-sparks from Rachmaninoff

or "Rock of Ages" or giving us
cascading "Autumn Leaves"

the way he loved to drive
around just him and me

Sunday afternoons singing
"Barbara Allen." In that

scarlet town where I was
born music was our dwelling.

O Daddy, I am leaning
on those everlasting arms.

SING OUT!

Tidying my office
I can't get the mandolin in its file
nor the black river in its banker's box.
I know I have to have a system
for everything
but what about the flute?
Does it go under *F* for its name
or *B* for bird, *W* for water music,
S for silver, *S* for seventh grader
which I was when
my finger pads first pressed
the cool dimpled buttons of its keys
first tucked my lower lip to make
a cliff of my upper lip
so that my breath would fill
the throat of the flute.
Or what about *T* for traded
which is what I did with the flute
one Saturday morning
at Cumberland Valley Music
after Joanie and I had our voice lesson
from Steeley Veech. I picked out
a guitar, its golden wooden promise
just what I wanted, not
lining up in maroon uniforms,
not marching, not halftime
football and the fight song and "O
say can you?" but black
turtlenecks and flowing skirts
and a black river of darkness
in the coffeehouse where, with long
hair flowing over my shoulder
down almost to the back
of my hand, picking "The Times
They Are A-Changing" I would
sing myself from state route 840

in Harlan County to Bleecker Street
in Greenwich Village and where
I'd meet the mandolin player
over from County Clare and where
he'd kiss me quick before we
went on, saying Your hair
shines like a black river.

MARY

When you were young
and lanky, graceful
bones visible, your wide
mouth and bright hair
made a vivid frame
for your voice.
On either side of you
dark-suited men
played guitars and sang,
their fingers dancing.

Your instrument
was that body.
A woman, you carried
the melody or high harmony
the descant, or low
weave of thirds and fifths
and beauty too.
You had to be beacon
virgin, siren
little girl, and vamp.
It comes to us at birth
this mantle—
no way to step onstage
without reference to it.

So you worked it,
shaking your hair
like a flag in the wind.
You were an actress after all.
No use to wear the mantle
like some ratty carpet remnant
when you could perfect
that dazzling twirl
managers, photographers,
and audiences swooned for.

It wasn't just the erotic
heat you bore like any
torch singer, but the shiny
energy advertising tomorrow
that rides a young woman's flesh.

In fact, you were already
a mother, your daughter
kept out of view. A grand-
mother now—heavy, clear
lines gone—you've survived
back surgeries, leukemia, bone
marrow transplant. Peter
and Paul, gray, thick, and bald
betray nothing. But you!
Some folks can't hear you
now because of what they
see, since your look was your
sound was your message round
and round the spindle
of image and desire.

Yes, your voice is lower, brassier
but Peter's and Paul's have
grown raspy, too, yet no website
bears their distorted pictures
like ones of you I found captioned
"Repulsive" and "Jabba the Hutt."
And you the same woman who helped
rally the "I Have a Dream" march,
who with mother and daughter
went to jail for protesting apartheid,
who gave your voice to changing
the times, to turning a nation.

These days you come onstage
with a cane and wavy sparse
after-chemo hair, bearing another
torch for us, the light of believing
anyway and laughing, the wise
slow steps of carrying it on.

TROUBADOUR

How Deborah came through the window
—well, she handed her banjo first—
of the kitchen in an apartment
that hangs off the side of a mountain

How she climbed through this break
in the Appalachian Writers Workshop
after the evenings' readings,
which were after our heavy supper,

which followed one-on-one conferences
sandwiched between workshops
planted so deep and thick and close
only a snake could get through

How she strode over the sill
when I lifted the screechy screen,
her brindled braid flying behind her
to lead us from the choke of talk

down to the well of song.

"WE'LL SEE THAT DAY COME 'ROUND"

Friday nights in high school when I didn't have a date
found me practicing guitar in my blue bedroom,
folk song books spread out around me, poets' words
I'd painted taped on the wall (Dylan Thomas, Thomas
Merton: I aspired to the condition of men). I learned
the other Dylan, sang after Joan Baez, picked Peter,
Paul and Mary, strummed my own tunes. Every chord
was progress toward protest on the Mall in Washington,
every wail might reach Greenwich Village and The Bitter
End. "I'm on my way," I sang. "Don't grieve after me."
"If you miss the train I'm on" and "All my bags
are packed." Music was my ticket out of the mountains
that gave it to me, out of myself, into an adulthood
so colosally cool that Woody Guthrie's "ribbon of highway"
would surely welcome me everywhere I went.
And if mine was "a long, lonesome road," well
I'd find song-swappers to be lonesome with
in the gatherings after great peace rallies or backstage
at Newport.
                  When Pete Seeger came to Harlan County
(the FBI right behind him), I sat at his feet
just like I froze on the Knoxville ice rink listening
to P P & M glorify the night with "Blowin' in the Wind,"
just like a couple of college years later I sat in the crow's nest
at Freedom Hall peering through pot haze (I wasn't smoking
but in that crowd, who needed to?) at Judy Collins's tiny
figure far away, her voice huge around us: "Amazing grace
how sweet the sound . . ." Marching, picketing,
I married a musician, then quit singing.
Now, having passed the speed limit (55)
some years back, I'm in a YMCA basement
mastering power chords with kids the age I was when
I traded my junior high flute for a guitar. And last week
at a memorial service for a civil rights hero, I led
the crowd in "We Shall Overcome." Memory, a few open

chords, and two-hundred people on their feet who had lived that song. *Honey,* I say to that Friday night self forty years back, *Don't think twice. It's alright.*

EVE OF WINTER

Against the silver rim of morning
      this very one
far below the eisenglass snip of moon
God places coral feather-cloud boas
piles them up like covers at the end
of the rich bed she just climbed out of.
God does not have to take a moon lantern
into the dark barn of night
and lean into the cow of chaos
to fetch us the milk of morning.
She does not have to tuck her flannel gown
into work pants and tunnel her great arms
into a weather-cracked mackinaw
and shimble down the frozen path
the way we do, tumbled from bed each dawn
to the kitchen barn, the coffee-colored coffee.

She could though. She could do it however
she would find *le plus amusant.*
She could tap dance on the guy wire for the phone pole
that bears the hoot owl light, God could.
She could get herself born in that barn if it pleased her.
Let there be, she says, every day of this
leafy leafless frozen flowering world
and there is, by God, there is is IS

IN THE BALANCE

Three phoebe fledglings
fling their feathered selves
over the woven rim of the nest,
glide—first try!—on new wings,
then land one-two-tree
on the same branch. Here
they lean in gray-green reunion.

But beyond this tree, the wide
sky is calling. And all
the wonder of the world
counts on these phoebes
to answer.

OAK

older
than I'll
ever be

apartment house
supermarket
factory

fashioning food
out of light

you were
the one word
acorn knew

Letting go
in the grave
it sprouted
and spoke:

Oak

INVENTING SIN

God signs to us
        We cannot read
She shouts
        We take cover
She shrugs
        and trains leave
        the tracks

Our schedules! we moan
Our loved ones

God is fed up

All the oceans She gave us
All the acres of steep seedful forests
And we did what
        Invented the Great Chain of Being
        and the chain saw
        Invented sin

God sees us now
        gorging ourselves
        and starving our neighbors
        starving ourselves
        and storing our grain
and She says

I've had it

        You cast your trash
        upon the waters
        It's rolling in

        You stuck your fine fine finger
        into the mystery of life
        to find death

and you did
Learned how to end the world
in nothing flat

Now you come crying
to your mommy
       Send us a miracle
       Prove that you exist
Look at your hand, I say
Listen to your scared heart
Do you have to haul the tide in
sweeten the berries on the vine

I set you down
a miracle among miracles
You want more—
It's your turn
You show me

I WANT TO SAY

I love the olive grove
Where Moshe and Amira were playing
Before the rocket hit

I love the well
The water of their lives
Was hauled up from

I love the llamas
Skin rubbed raw
From mortar rounds
Strapped to their matted sides

I love the tear streaks
On the dusty neck
Of the father home from the front
Clutching his children's bodies to his chest

I love the heartbeat of hope
When he might admit
That he killed children today

I love the inbreath
Before
He cries vengeance.

PRAYER

Our Mother Who Art
in the kitchen
cooking us up
hallowed may we see
all that is
Your kingdom here
delivered into our hands
Your will in children
and trees leafing out
on earth
as if it were Heaven.

Give us this day
bread we could feed
the world
and snatch us bald-headed
if we try to swallow it all.

Don't forgive us
till we learn it is all for giving.
That salve you've got in a pot
on the back of the stove
only heals when everybody has some.

And heed us not
if we believe You look like us
and love us best
and gave us the True Truth
with a license to kill Others
writ inside.
Deliver us from this evil.

For it is Yours,
this kitchen we call Universe
where you stir up our favorite treat,
the Milky Way,

folding deep into sweet
our little sphere
with its powerful glory
     of rainforests
     and oceans
     and mountains in feather-boa mist
forever
     if we don't blow it up
     and ever
     if we don't tear it down
Amen

(Ah women
Ah children
Ah reckon She's about fed up.
We better make room at the table
for everybody
before She yells "OUT!"
and turns our table over,
before She calls it off
this banquet we've been hoarding
this paradise
we aim to save
with bombs.)

DEAREST

these things happen.
I need you to call me
when the eye passes over.
Don't stand near the window.
Just take off the ring I gave you
slip it in your mouth
and no matter how loud
the stillness
no matter what inside room
you are crouching in
I will know it's you
calling.
I will get in my dream
and be right over.
You mean that much to me.

MEETING THE NOTEBOOK

The notebook is bigger than I am.
Every two-sided page has its cutting edge.

Open, its facing pages lie
large as a snow-covered garden

blue lines, pale
as the veins in my breasts.

I must enter this empty order
with my chaos

I who am already
thumbed-through, full.

The notebook does not know
I am its history

but it is bound
to find out.

POULTRY

Hunt and peck,
my little chickens.
Make good layers.
Then brood
upon the true work
of the nest:

to warm that stone
till you see yourself
in it, your silly self
reborn, in fine feather,
bright-eyed, with a pair
of singing

wings.

AT TALLAND HOUSE

—Where Virginia Woolf spent her childhood
summers, the setting of *To the Lighthouse*

Godrevy Light
cut across me.
It blessed and blinded
and bound me,
wound me in its skein of light
the way a spider silks in her prey

and there I hung, glittering
on a web in the escallonia—
that hedge you Stephen children
cut through on your way to the beach.
(Laughing, outrunning Adrian,
you try to catch up with Vanessa,
a butterfly just above your shoulder.)

Or perhaps, pilgrim soul,
perhaps I am not trapped
waiting to be devoured
but cocooned by this force
that weaves your life into mine

till the self that only crawled dissolves
to spin something wholly new—
blue-winged and iridescent—

a flying flower hovering in the hedge
till the next time you rush through.

TO SAY NOTHING OF YOUR FACE

—Looking at a photograph

I see that you wear a little finger ring
and your long hands are not thin as I
supposed but full and strong in 1934.
You are fifty-two, three years
younger than I am now, the tie
of your paisley silk blouse loose-
knotted, the lapels of your dark
velvet jacket disappearing into
the black of the negative. Because
the background is white, because
of contrast, detail can be lost.
But I see your watch. With a magnifier,
I can even see the time: it's four o'clock,
Virginia. When you are finished
looking at me, seventy years on,
will you have tea? Then let a London walk
ease your evening? Lift of November streets,
squares of history factoring you back
into the world Man Ray so
famously snapped you out of.

FOUR STONE STEPS

I

Sixty summers
after you made the river your bed,
I came to stay
in the nursery at Talland House.
From Kentucky
I had planned and plotted to arrive,
husband and teenage son in tow,
at the site of *that great Cathedral*
space which was childhood.

Car trip, flight delay, train trek,
and by midnight we were there
—"shattered by travel" as the cabbie said—
taking our first meal of bread, cheese,
and wine in the little kitchen.

Effervescent with the moment,
I read aloud your words:
Our house, Talland House
. . . had . . . so many corners
and lawns that each was named.
"She means *here*," I said.
"She lived in these rooms."
"Yeah, Mom. Would you
pass the cheese?"

2

The next morning,
by gulls and waves awakened,
I closed the door
on sleeping males
and went down in lemon light
to your mother's garden,
its white lattice trellis

woven around on O,
the *os* from which all things come.

Passion flower, primrose,
alyssum, astilbe
crowd the four stone steps
down to *the love corner,*

the coffee garden, the cricket
ground, the Lookout.

Here they brought you,
seven months old, in August 1882.
Servants and nurses,
                    Leslie and Julia,
three adolescents,
                    three children under six
(and a dog) ·
all sweltering
in layers of fine summer cloth
changing trains at St. Erth
and steaming on the branch line
down to Cornwall,
which your father called
"the very toenail of England."

The hem of your mother's
dressing gown is wet
with dew, her teacup
rattles on the balcony.

And you settled into
that summer and summers
after, learned to walk
down the four stone steps
around which your mother's

flowers flourished, learned
to swim, thrown naked
by your father into the sea.

Here you caught moths
and played cricket
and lowered a basket
at night out the nursery
window, hoping Sophie the cook
would send up something
vouchsafed from
the grown-up's dinner. Some-
times she did, sometimes
she cut the string. So
your mother was
snipped from this life
in your thirteenth spring
her departing words,
"Hold yourself
straight, my little Goat."

You touched the cold iron of her face
before they carried what was left
down steep
        dark
    narrow
          zigzag
   stairs.
The door closed on Talland House too.

Only words let you live here again,
words that summoned me,
words that break this moment
on the shore and rise, incense
from the garden.

3

Night at the nursery window
and Godrevy Light sweeps
the garden, its four stone steps
like tombstones for bereft children
Thoby
     Vanessa
          Adrian
               Virginia
your father pitched
down the well of grief
and you, Ginny, left shattered,
up for grabs.

4

A hundred and six summers
since your mother's death
and still the weight
of those steps, like stones
in your pockets
on the last afternoon of your life
drags me down
to a point so still
stone breathes

and I am held
out of time
in darkness
till the tide turns
till peach light
over waves breaking
and gulls crying,
"Keep! Keep! Keep! Keep!"
and "Try! Try! Try!"
brings me back

to dawn
in your mother's garden
a ghost
among ghosts
in full bloom.

TO VIRGINIA

If you knew
I sat
at your feet

    I think you do know

If you'd seen me
retrace your steps
Hyde Park Gate   *where you were born*
Gordon Square   *birthplace of Bloomsbury*
Asheham   now a cement works
Monk's House   *last home*

    perhaps you did see

If you'd watched
your words
light my darkness
like the Milky Way

If you'd felt me
pouring over
leaning into
your diary
and *To the Lighthouse*
and *Jacob's Room*

boarding an aeroplane
to cross the Atlantic
catching a train
from Paddington
to St Ives
to stay in the nursery
at Talland House,
sacred site
of your childhood summers

before your mother's death
slammed that gate

If you'd heard me
reading aloud your words
in that room where you drew
your baby breaths
and blew bubbles of words,
where you were translated by time
into a fierce, dreamy, always
ink-stained girl

would you have said
do you say

Welcome, daughter?

FROM THE PAGE

I am blank
because your heart
is scrawled over with stories.

I am empty
because your life is full.

I am perfectly flat
so you can pitch a tent
      a fit
          a high sweet song.

I am light
so you can make your mark.

I am open
so you can walk in.

Lean close.
Let me feel your breath.
Ah!
Tell me everything.

THAT NIGHT

in Florence when I couldn't sleep for tears
torn out of me, when I couldn't breathe
for what felt like a man-hole cover crushing
my heart, I knew that I could die of my own
limitations, that I *would* die, as we all do,
of just that, and I prayed as the iron disc
bore down and I dragged each breath
out from under: Great Mother, I give up, give in
to whatever it takes to raise this weight.
Let me die of wounds and not armor.

RELEASE

I am taking off my father's brace,
leather-covered metal basket
that aligned his spine and made his back
work. I'm tugging the canvas straps
out of their silver buckles. With a clink
and a jingle, they pull free. I'm lifting
harness off plump, dented shoulders,
separating sweat-stained lattice
from freckled back. I'm setting it
down now, that salty apparatus.
It stands by itself, my father
long gone.

SHE LET HERSELF GO

1.

She let herself go   soft   fat   sexual   She let herself go to the library to college to extremes   She let herself go wild   and gray   and all the way   She let herself go deep go alone   go sane   She let herself stay   She let herself abide by her own rules   She let herself out   She let herself in   Let herself in for it   She put down her mask   She held out her arms   She let herself go

2.

She let herself go far   go ahead   go overboard   without saying   without apology without   She undid her bra   peeled off her hose   let herself breathe   She let herself fill up with air   no matter who was threatened   by the swell of her belly   She let herself go around with her own face no foundation concealer minimizer   She let herself be   She left dishes in the sink   dust furring Great Aunt Sudie's breakfront   Seeing her neighbors' manicured lawn, she thought   Don't they have anything to read?

3.

She let herself have her limits   her bad points   her life   She discovered she was Some Body   not just Any Body   not an object of fashion fantasy failure   But a woman—not a doll cellophane-worshipped flung to the back of the closet purchased to be perfect

92

forgotten under the bed   And she let herself change   things besides diapers   what's in the refrigerator   the state of the floor   She changed   She made change   She thought of herself for a change   She let herself flow   and there were stains and cramps and shit and shouting in driveways and walking out   fear grinding the guts   tears tearing down the freeway   the free   way

4.

Letting herself go   and come   She came to the end of her rope and hung on though she'd learned to let go   till her numb hand sprung and she fell backward   turning over and almost inside out   landing in the pit of grief   the lap of light   open mouth wailing   open arms welcoming   smashed by the rock soothed by the rocking   She's through!   She's through!   Into the abyss   Into bliss   a twist   at the end of the road   a translation   dark night become the radiant way   She let herself go.

93

7